VICTORIAN LIFE

A VICTORIAN SCHOOL

Wayland

VICTORIAN LIFE

A VICTORIAN CHRISTMAS

A VICTORIAN FACTORY

A VICTORIAN HOLIDAY

A VICTORIAN SCHOOL

A VICTORIAN STREET

A VICTORIAN SUNDAY

VICTORIAN CLOTHES

VICTORIAN TRANSPORT

HOW WE LEARN ABOUT THE VICTORIANS

Queen Victoria reigned from 1837 to 1901, a time when Britain went through enormous social and industrial changes. We can learn about Victorians in various ways. We can still see many of their buildings standing today, we can look at their documents, maps and artefacts – many of which can be found in museums. Photography, invented during Victoria's reign, gives us a good picture of life in Victorian Britain. In this book you will see what Victorian life was like through some of this historical evidence.

With thanks to Matthew Baptie at the History of Education Centre, Edinburgh for his help.

This edition published in 1994 by Wayland (Publishers) Ltd

First published in 1993 by Wayland (Publishers) Ltd, 61 Western Road, Hove, East Sussex BN3 1JD, England

© Copyright 1993 Wayland (Publishers) Ltd

British Library Cataloguing in Publication Data
Wood, Richard
  Victorian School. - (Victorian Life Series)
  I. Title II. Series
  370.941

HARDBACK ISBN 0-7502-0690-X
PAPERBACK ISBN 0-7502-1370-1

Printed and bound in Italy by G. Canale & C. S.p.A.

Series design: Pardoe Blacker Ltd
Editor: Sarah Doughty

Cover picture: A school group photograph from 1885.

Picture acknowledgements
Mary Evans 7, 8, 9 (top), 11, 23 (top), 24, 25 (bottom), 27; Greater London Photo Library 6, 12 (bottom), 18, 19, 22; J. Allan Cash Ltd 9 (bottom); Mansell Collection 4; Archie Miles (cover); National Trust Photo Library (Mike Williams) 6 (top); Northamptonshire Libraries and Information Service 20; Victoria and Albert Museum 5 (top); Richard Wood 5 (bottom).

Thanks to Norfolk Museums Service for supplying items from their museums on pages 10 (both), 12 (top), 13 (both), 14, 15 (both), 17 (both), 21 (top), 23 (bottom), 25 (top), 26 (both), and to Barnham Broom Primary School for supplying the timetable on page 16.

All commissioned photography by GGS Photo Graphics.

CONTENTS

SCHOOLS FOR THE MANY

How many years will you be at school? Today, British children spend at least eleven years in primary and secondary schools. In early Victorian England some poor children never went to school. Most only attended for a few years, if they were lucky enough. Later on, many new schools were started. Laws were passed so all children had to go to school until they were ten.

A FACTORY SCHOOL

Instead of going to school, many poor children in early Victorian Britain worked for low wages in factories or on farms. Some wealthy people thought that school would make children unhappy and hard to control. They did not want them to read books that criticized the way the country was run. But other people, like Manchester cotton trader Robert Owen, thought that a simple schooling would be useful.

A dancing lesson at Robert Owen's factory school, 1823.

Robert Owen took his ideas to Scotland where he set up a school at his cotton mills in New Lanark in 1817. Here the children learned how to read and write. They also had singing and dancing lessons.

A DAME SCHOOL

There were few chances for most poor children to go to school, except to the charity schools. Parents with a few pence to spare could send their children to Dame schools. But some of the women who ran Dame schools could not even read for themselves! In Scotland, there were parish schools which provided education for poor children.

A teacher teaching in a Dame school.

In 1844, new laws were passed saying that children working in factories should be given six half-days' schooling every week. Ragged schools were opened in some towns to give free education to very poor children.

NATIONAL SCHOOLS

Many churches ran Sunday schools to teach children to read the Bible. Some opened weekday schools called National or British schools.

Barnham Broom National School, opened 1841.

From 1833, these schools could apply for money from the government to help with costs. Sometimes new schools were built. But often the schoolroom was in a church, a cottage, or even an old barn.

SCHOOLS
FOR THE FEW

Boys and girls from better-off English families did not mix with poor children. Middle-class boys went to local grammar schools, or to private schools. Others went away to boarding schools. Girls and boys did not attend the same schools. There were few girls' schools, so rich girls often had private tutors at home.

EDUCATION AT HOME

Middle-class children often began their school days at home. They were taught how to read and write by their mothers, or by a nanny. Sometimes they were sent to small private schools in other people's houses instead. Many rich girls had a governess who was paid to teach them subjects like needlework and French, and they went to private tutors for music and dancing.

A governess teaching children.

PUBLIC SCHOOLS

Rich boys often went away to board at public schools like Eton when they were about 10 years old. These older schools taught Classics (Latin and Greek). This was to prepare boys to

Eton College school yard.

go to university. Life at school was often hard. Young boys became fags (servants) for older boys, who often bullied them. The government became worried about the public schools and ordered a report on them in 1868. Slowly the schools became better run and the boys properly cared for.

Lancing College, founded in 1849.

Many new public schools, like Lancing College in Sussex, opened from the 1840s. These schools tried to develop the boys' characters through religion, sport and good discipline. Less time was spent on learning Latin, and subjects like English, science and music were introduced.

PRIVATE SCHOOLS

There were also many private schools for middle-class children. Many were good schools. Others were very poor, with few books and unhealthy buildings. Charles Dickens' novel *Nicholas Nickleby* describes life at an imaginary school called Dotheboys Hall with its cruel headmaster, Mr Squeers. Many people were shocked by the story, and tried to improve such schools. *Tom Brown's Schooldays* is another famous Victorian school story. The author, Thomas Hughes, described Rugby public school, where the headmaster, Dr. Arnold, wanted his pupils to become good people as well as good students.

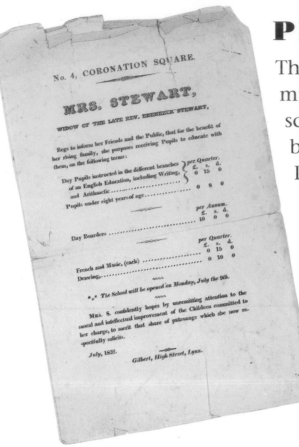

An advertisement for a small private school.

GRAMMAR SCHOOLS

Many towns had day grammar schools for boys up to sixteen or eighteen years old. These had been started hundreds of years before to give free education to boys. By Victorian times they charged high fees. Only boys from well-off families could afford to attend. At first, Latin and Greek grammar were the only subjects on the timetable. Later, other languages such as French were taught, as well as maths and science, sometimes for extra fees. On the right is a page from a language teaching book.

A French and German language teaching book.

SCHOOLS FOR GIRLS

There were not many schools for middle-class girls until late Victorian times. For centuries, marriage and domestic life had been the only way of life for women. After 1870, however, grammar schools started separate sections for girls. Many new private girls' schools also opened. They taught art and music, sewing and cookery, elocution (good speech) and manners. Parents hoped these subjects would help their daughters to find rich husbands.

Schoolgirls from a private school.

THE THREE RS

The three Rs were Reading, wRiting and aRithmetic. Most school children learned these subjects every day. The Victorians thought they were more important than other subjects like history, science and music. Religion was another R that boys and girls had to learn. Inspectors visited schools every year to test children on the three Rs.

READING LESSON

First, children learned to read and write the letters of the alphabet. When they knew the sound of each letter, they put letters together to make simple words. They may have begun with short words like 'fish', 'dish' and 'wish'. Then they went on to longer ones like 'fishing', 'dishes' and 'swished'. Sometimes the teacher drew pictures and words on the blackboard for the children to copy. These helped them remember the words they learned.

The infants' reading lesson at a London Board school.

WRITING AND DICTATION

Paper was expensive, so children usually wrote on slates. The slates were often fixed in wooden frames, but they broke very easily if they were dropped. Sometimes they were marked with lines. These helped children to write straight and keep all their letters the same size. They wrote with slate pencils, thin sticks of slate sharpened to a point.

The children often copied the words or sums that the teacher wrote on the blackboard. Sometimes the teacher read out a passage from a book which the children wrote down. This was called 'dictation'. After the slates were checked, the children were told to wipe their slates clean.

Slate with slate pencil.

PENS AND INK

Older children learned to write on paper as well as slates. A boy or girl called the 'ink monitor' poured a little black or blue ink into the ink wells on the desks. Pens, which were like thin wooden sticks with scratchy steel needles were handed out. When the teacher gave the order, the children dipped these in the ink and began to write. They had to dip the nibs after every few words or the pens would run dry.

Pen, ink bottle and inkwells.

HANDWRITING

All children learned to write the same sort of
'copperplate' handwriting. Copy books had a
sentence already written or printed at the top of
each page. Usually it was a proverb, or a useful
piece of information like 'India is seven times
bigger than Great Britain'. This was copied on
to blank lines underneath. The size and shape
of the letters had to be exactly the same.
Children were careful not to 'blot their
copybooks' with blobs of ink.

A page from a Victorian school
copy book.

ARITHMETIC

Arithmetic was the third R. The youngest
children used 'ball frames' with coloured beads
to learn how to add and take away numbers.
Older children learned how to multiply and
divide. They often had to do simple sums in
their heads. This was called 'mental arithmetic'.
They also had to do sums with money.

In old money there were twelve pennies (12d) in one shilling (1s) and twenty shillings (20/-) in a pound (£1).

Children also had to know weights like ounces, pounds, stones and hundredweights, and measures like pints, gallons, pecks and bushels. The metric system we use today is much simpler than the Victorian 'imperial' measures. Here is an example of the arithmetic they had to do. Can you see how they calculated this difficult sum?

Pupils' counting frames.

Examples

If 11 lb. of sugar cost 9 s. 6 d what will 123 lb cost?

As 11 : 9 . 6 :: 123

```
        12
      1 1 4
          4
      4 5 6
      1 2 3
    1 3 6 8
      9 1 2
      4 5 6
11) 5 6 0 4 8
 4) 5 0 9 8 - 10
12) 1 2 7 4 - ½
2,0) 1 0 . 6 - 2
     5" 6" 2½ - 10. Ans
```

A sum to work out the price of sugar.

WORK AND
PLAY

How many different things do you do at school? You probably study several subjects every day. You may have projects and topics as well as games and playtime. Victorian children were not so lucky. They did the same things every day. The teacher watched the class from a raised desk. Children sat in long silent rows facing the teacher. School was not meant to be fun.

Timetable for Barnham Broom National School, 1874.

This village school timetable was written by the teacher and signed by a school inspector. Every day began with prayers, then religious instruction. The rest of the day was spent on the three Rs, apart from some geography, singing and girls' sewing.

A CATECHISM

This geography book has no pictures. It is called a catechism because it instructs by questions and answers. The children learned the questions and answers by heart. They learned many facts by rote. Lists of names, places, or weights and measures were chanted aloud over and over again until they remembered them.

OBJECT LESSONS

Sometimes the teacher gave an 'object lesson'. This object box has five trays of tiny samples for children to see. They include pieces of stone, seeds, shells and fabrics. Topics for infants' object lessons included 'the turnip', 'a jug', 'baby frogs' and 'uses of the cow'.

Object lesson readers were class books with illustrations. Object lesson cards were mounted on the wall for children to look at after the lesson.

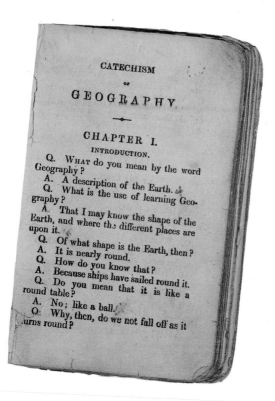

Geography textbook.

Object box for an object lesson.

PHYSICAL EDUCATION

Girls doing drill in a London school playground, about 1900.

Physical education lessons were called 'drill'. When the teacher shouted orders, all the children marched or swung their arms the same way. Drill taught children to obey orders quickly and without thinking. When it was very cold they did drill indoors to keep warm. If there was a piano, drill was sometimes done to music. Some teachers gave orders by shouting out numbers. Here is a list from one school:

One! Stand in desk
Two! Put left leg over seat
Three! Put right leg over seat
Four! Face the door
Five! March on the spot
Six! Step forward

PLAYTIME

Most schools had a small playground for the children to use during breaks. One girl remembered, 'We only had the yard around the school for play. It was very rough, just loose soil, and we got very dirty. There was no tap so we washed in the stream that ran down the street.' Toilets were in outside sheds. They were usually just a row of seats over a pit in the ground.

For games, the iron hoop shown here could be rolled round the playground with the stick. Other popular playtime games were tiddlywinks, hopscotch and skipping to rhymes like this:

'Georgie Ware is a very good man
He teaches his children all he can
To read and write and arithmetic
And didn't forget to give them the stick...'

Playtime at a Welsh Board school, about 1900.

TEACHERS
AND PUPILS

Would your teacher want 500 children to teach? Some Victorian teachers had even more pupils than that. They were helped by monitors, who were boys and girls aged between about 9 and 11. Later on, classes became smaller. Older 'pupil teachers' replaced the monitors. Most Victorian teachers were not trained. Life was often hard for teachers as well as pupils.

THE MONITORIAL SYSTEM

The idea of having monitors to teach younger children began in the church schools. It was a cheap system because few adults were needed. The head teacher taught the monitors. Then they passed on what they were told to the younger children, who were taught in groups. It was a poor method of learning, as many monitors could hardly read or write themselves.

PUPIL TEACHERS

From 1846, 'pupil teachers' often replaced monitors. There were five year apprenticeships for boys and girls aged over thirteen who had left school. They were paid about three shillings (15p) a week to help teach the 'standards'. Their work was closely watched by teachers and inspectors. If they did well they could become qualified teachers when they were 18.

After 1832, some colleges started to train teachers. But most teachers, especially in country schools, were never trained. Teachers' pay was poor, but Board School teachers were often given a free house next to the school. Under the parish school system in Scotland, teachers were given two rooms above or next to the school, a garden and an acre of land.

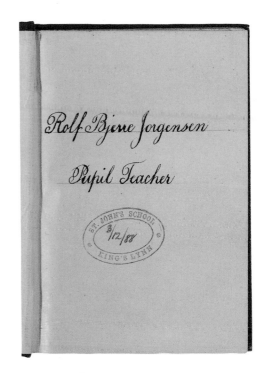

A pupil teacher's notebook, 1888.

Swannington country school, about 1900.

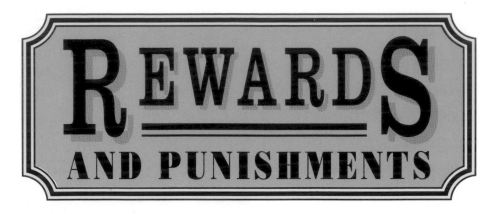

REWARDS
AND PUNISHMENTS

Do you enjoy school? Most of us do, at least some of the time. Modern schools are usually happy, friendly places. But in Victorian times teachers were very strict. There was no talking in lessons and the work was often difficult and dull. However, if children attended school every day and worked hard, they were given rewards. If they were lazy or late or badly behaved, they were punished.

THE SCHOOL INSPECTOR

After 1839, many schools were given money by the government. These schools were visited every year by an inspector who checked the standard of teaching by the staff. He looked at the school building, the equipment and checked the timetable and registers. Then he tested all the children, one by one, on their reading, writing and arithmetic. Those who passed the inspector's test were allowed to move up to the next standard.

A school inspector testing children.

REWARDS

Some schools gave prizes, medals or certificates to encourage children to work hard. This certificate was given to a pupil for religious knowledge. 'Payment by Results' began in 1862. This meant that the amount of money each school received depended on the pupils' results in the annual tests. This was very unpopular with teachers, who were paid less if the children's work was poor. But some 'class subjects' could earn extra money for the school.

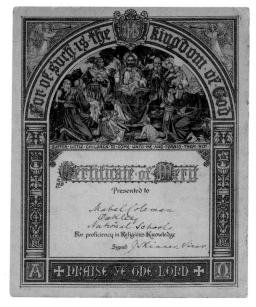

A certificate awarded for good work.

THE 'DUNCE' OF THE CLASS

Children who could not remember their lessons, or did bad work, were called dunces. Sometimes teachers made them stand by the wall wearing a tall, pointed hat. Unkind pupils made fun of 'the dunce of the class'.

The dunce in the corner.

GOOD ATTENDANCE

Rewards were given to children who never missed school. Inspectors checked up on attendances during the year. If there were many absences, the school's grant money was reduced. However, some children were often absent when sick. Others took days off to go bird scaring, help with farmwork or gather firewood, fruit or nuts. In Leith in Scotland, the School Board received a complaint that Board members were employing boys as golf caddies when they should have been at school.

A medal for good attendance.

GOOD RESULTS

This card was given to James Boughton to show that he had passed the 'fourth standard'. He was only ten, but was allowed to leave school. To pass his test, James had to read from a book, write down a passage dictated by the inspector, and do some arithmetic.

Children who failed had to try again the next year. This meant that some children in each class were much older than others.

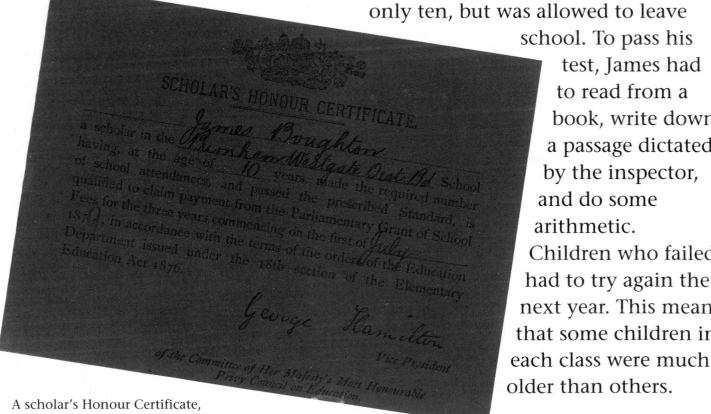

A scholar's Honour Certificate, 1879.

DISCIPLINE

Victorian parents and teachers were often very strict. Most people believed that children who were naughty or lazy should be caned. Scottish teachers used a leather strap called a tawse. The children expected the teacher to be strict. The writer, Flora Thompson, described what happened when a teacher tried to be friendly to her class. The children thought she was weak. They hid her cane, filled her inkpot with water, put frogs in her desk and coughed loudly when she spoke. Children, as well as teachers, could be cruel.

A cruel thrashing.

GLOSSARY

Apprenticeship A way of training young people at work to do a particular job.

Attendance Officer A man whose job was to make sure that children went to school.

Board School An elementary school run by an elected Board of Governors.

Boarding school A school where pupils also live during term time.

Caddies People who carry clubs and balls for golf players.

Classics The study of the ancient Latin and Greek languages.

Copperplate A style of joined-up handwriting with thin sloping letters.

Dame school A small private school run by a teacher in her own home.

Elementary school A school that taught simple subjects to children aged under 14.

Governess A woman employed to teach the children of one family in their own home.

Grammar The rules of language.

Imperial measures Old measurements, like feet and inches, pints and quarts.

Infants The youngest school children, aged 4 to 6.

Inspector of Schools A man whose job was to check up on schools, teachers and pupils.

Log Book A diary of all the main happenings at a school.

Metric system Measurements like metres and litres, which can be divided by ten.

Monitor Usually an older pupil who was put in charge of younger ones.

Nanny Someone who looks after young children.

National school An elementary school run by a church.

Private school A fee-paying school, run for profit.

Proverb A well-known saying such as, 'Too many cooks spoil the broth'.

Public school A large fee-paying school that was originally set up as a charity.

Ragged school A charity school for very poor children.

Rote learning Learning things by heart by saying them over and over again.

Slate Soft grey stone that can be split into thin sheets for writing on.

Standards The average level of work that can be done by children at a certain age. Also, a class of children working at the same level.

BOOKS TO READ

Harper, R. *Finding Out About Victorian Childhood* (Batsford, 1986)

Purkiss, S. *Exploring Schools* (Wayland, 1988)

Ross, S. *Our Schools* (Wayland, 1992)

Speed, P. *Learning and Teaching in Victorian Times* (Longman, 1988)

Steel, A. *Victorian Children* (Wayland, 1990)

Stoppleman, M. *School Day* (A & C Black, 1985)

Tanner, G. and Wood, T. *History Mysteries – At School* (A & C Black, 1992)

PLACES TO VISIT

Many museums have displays about Victorian schools. Sometimes it is possible to arrange handling or role play sessions. Those listed below all have reconstructed Victorian classrooms.

ENGLAND

Cambridgeshire: Centre For Environmental Education, Stibbington, Peterborough, PE8 6LP. Tel. 0780 782386

Cheshire: Heritage Centre, Roe Street, Macclesfield, SK11 6UT. Tel. 0625 613210

Quarry Bank Mill, Styal, SK9 4LA. Tel. 0625 527468

County Durham: North of England Open Air Museum, Beamish, DH9 ORG. Tel. 0207 231811

Hertfordshire: British Schools Museum, Queen Street, Hitchin, SG4 9TS. Tel. 0462 422946

Lancashire: Museum of Childhood, Lancaster, LA1 1YS. Tel. 0524 32808

Wigan Pier Heritage Centre, Wigan, WN3 4EU. Tel. 0942 323666

London: Ragged School Museum, Copperfield Road, London, E3 4RR. Tel. 071 232 2941

Merseyside: Museum of Labour History, Islington, L3 8EE. Tel. 051 207 0001

Norfolk: Gressenhall Rural Life Museum, Dereham, NR20 4DR. Tel. 0362 860563

Oxfordshire: Fringford Old School, Woodstock, OX7 1SN. Tel. 0993 811456

Staffordshire: Country Museum, Shugborough, ST17 OXB. Tel. 0889 881388

Sussex: Weald and Downland Museum, Singleton, PO18 OEU. Tel. 024363 348

Warwickshire: St.Johns House Museum, Warwick, CV34 4NF. Tel. 0926 412034

Worcestershire: Tudor House Museum, Worcester, WR1 2NA. Tel. 0905 355071

Yorkshire: Industrial Museum, Eccleshill, Bradford, BD2 3HP. Tel. 0274 631756

Leeds Industrial Museum, Armley, LS12 2QF. Tel. 0532 797326

SCOTLAND

Angus: Angus Folk Museum, Glamis, Forfar, DD8 1RT. Tel. 037 84288

Edinburgh: History of Education Centre, East London Street, Edinburgh, EH7 4BW. Tel. 031 556 4224

Glasgow: Museum of Education, Scotland Street, G5 8QB. Tel. 041 429 1202

Lanark: New Lanark Mills, ML11 9DB. Tel. 0555 61345

WALES

Cardiff: Welsh Folk Museum, St. Fagans, CF5 6XB. Tel. 0222 569441

NORTHERN IRELAND

County Down: Ulster Folk and Transport Museum, Holywood, BT18 OEU. Tel. 0232 428428

County Tyrone: Ulster American Folk Park, Castletown, Omagh, BT78 5QY. Tel. 0662 243292

INDEX